PRAYER OR MANTRA?

A Contrast Between Christian Prayer and Eastern Meditation

David G. Smithson, M.D.

Unity Library & Archives
1901 NW Blue Parkway
Unity Village, MO 64065

Seventy-Three Publications
SHAWNEE MISSION, KANSAS

© 2006 David Smithson. Printed and bound in the United States of America. All rights reserved. No part of this book may be reproduced or transmitted in any form or by any means, electronic or mechanical, including photocopying, recording, or by an information storage and retrieval system—except by a reviewer who may quote brief passages in a review to be printed in a magazine, newspaper, or on the Web—without permission in writing from the publisher. For information, please contact Seventy-Three Publications, PO Box 23207, Shawnee Mission, KS 66283.

Although the author and publisher have made every effort to ensure the accuracy and completeness of information contained in this book, we assume no responsibility for errors, inaccuracies, omissions, or any inconsistency herein. Any slighting of people, places, or organizations is unintentional.

First printing 2006
ISBN-13: 978-0-9776211-3-2
ISBN-10: 0-9776211-3-8
LCCN: 2006900020

ATTENTION CORPORATIONS, UNIVERSITIES, COLLEGES, AND PROFESSIONAL ORGANIZATIONS: Quantity discounts are available on bulk purchases of this book for educational, gift purposes, or as premiums for increasing magazine subscriptions or renewals. Special books or book excerpts can also be created to fit specific needs. For information, please contact Seventy-Three Publications, PO Box 23207, Shawnee Mission, KS 66283; 816-943-4629.

*To my wife Mollie:
my best friend, my confidant,
and my love.*

*To our children:
for being such a joy
in our lives.*

TABLE OF CONTENTS

About the Author vi

Preface vii

Acknowledgments ix

1. **Starting the Journey** 1
2. **Mind and Body** 4
3. **The Meditation Model** 17
4. **Crossing the Bridge** 24
5. **On the Other Side** 40
6. **Personhood—A Key Difference** 43
7. **The Eastern Invasion of the West** 46
8. **The Eastern Invasion Repackaged** 54
9. **Just Another "High"?** 62
10. **Spiritual Combat** 70
11. **The Supernatural Flight** 73

Notes 77

Index....................................... 81

ABOUT THE AUTHOR

Born in Winona, Minnesota, David G. Smithson, M.D., graduated summa cum laude from St. Mary's University of Minnesota with degrees in chemistry and biology. He worked in laboratory research at the Mayo Clinic in Rochester and graduated from medical school at the University of Minnesota in Minneapolis. His medicine/surgery internship was completed at the Gundersen Clinic/LaCrosse Lutheran Hospital in LaCrosse, Wisconsin. He then went on to finish a residency in the specialty of physical medicine and rehabilitation at the University of Washington in Seattle. Dr. Smithson is board certified in physical medicine and rehabilitation. He has practiced the last fifteen years in the Kansas City area and is currently the director of an inpatient medical rehabilitation ward at a large hospital there. His medical practice involves the rehabilitative care of stroke, brain injured, spinal cord injured, orthopedic, and other patients.

Dr. Smithson lives with his wife and their five children in the greater Kansas City area. He enjoys jogging, basketball, and spending time with his family. This is his first book.

PREFACE

The idea for this book actually started in a grocery store. While waiting in line at the checkout aisle a glance at the nearby magazine rack caught my eye. It was there that I saw a *Time* magazine cover article titled "The Science of Meditation." On the cover was a woman sitting with her eyes closed and legs crossed in the classic eastern meditation position. Picking it up I noted an interesting picture inside of a Tibetan monk undergoing brain imaging. I was intrigued. As a physician in the field of physical medicine and rehabilitation, I care daily for stroke and brain injured patients. I review brain-imaging studies and correlate the individual results with each patient's function. As I stood there in the grocery store, holding the magazine, various questions passed through my mind: What happens in the brain during meditation? What happens during prayer? What is the difference between meditation and prayer? My interest was piqued, and I was sold. The magazine was purchased along with the other groceries.

It was later that evening when I again picked up the *Time* magazine. Although the article was primarily about eastern meditation there were also three brief references to Christian meditation and prayer. I pondered further questions: What are the differences between eastern meditation and Christian meditation? What about the differences between Christian meditation and Christian prayer? What is the relationship between eastern religious beliefs and Christian beliefs in all of this? I decided to find out more.

Thus started the process of research and writing over more than a two-year span that eventually resulted in this book. The process involved late afternoons spent in the hospital medical library looking up journal articles or other related references. It also involved many early mornings reviewing related articles in the lay press, Old or New Testament writings, Buddhist passages, Internet search results, and so forth. There was reading and rereading, writing and rewriting.

Is this short little book an all-encompassing thesis on the topics of meditation and prayer? Of course not. Does it instead look at the subject matter in new and fascinating ways? Does it intrigue and even challenge? That is my hope.

In the final analysis this book was written for the serious general reader who has an interest in the topics of meditation and prayer. It is not written as a textbook but as a journey. Let the journey begin!

ACKNOWLEDGMENTS

My gratitude and thanks to:

My wife, Mollie, for her insights and considerable patience in helping to make this book a reality.

My brother, Doug, whose input regarding the issue of personhood helped shape the book.

Mike Steber, for the support and banter of ideas.

Carolyn, for her transcription assistance during the earlier stages, and Edwina, for her secretarial assistance throughout.

Isabella and Michelle, for their continued encouragement, valuable input, and prayerful support.

Jan Foster, whose cheerful medical library assistance was invaluable.

Nancy Sipley, whose excellent editorial skills and input were most helpful.

The many friends, colleagues, and interested people who read and critiqued the book during its multiple developmental stages.

1 Starting the Journey

If one says "Jesus" over and over again, is it a prayer or a mantra?

What about meditation strictly as stress management? Are there any potential problems?

What happened in Jesus' brain when he prayed?

Is "nonreligious" meditation really nonreligious?

Imagine the following: On the one hand, let's say that a Christian goes off to a quiet place to begin to pray. Once off at the quiet place, he may read some Bible verses or contemplate on some of Christ's teachings. He closes his eyes and gets into a comfortable sitting position or possibly a kneeling position as he is focusing more and more on Christ and his teachings. He starts to quietly pray.

On the other hand, another person who practices eastern meditation goes off to a quiet place in order to meditate. Once at this quiet place he may sit down with his legs crossed in front of him. He also closes his eyes and begins to calm his mind. He starts to quietly meditate.

From an external perspective, these two would seem to be very similar. If we looked at them they would both be silent, with eyes closed, focused on their own individual thoughts, impervious to the outside surroundings. Where are they? Are they on some type of journey?

This is a book about meditation and prayer. The topic itself could be considered under the newly emerging discipline of neurotheology, which is the relationship of the spiritual to the workings of the brain. In this book we contrast what happens when one prays in the Christian sense versus meditating in the eastern sense. Within this contrast some of the points developed are as follows:

- Health benefits as well as potential side effects of eastern meditation versus Christian prayer.
- A current prayer and meditation model is reviewed, describing differences between Christian prayer and eastern meditation.
- Issue of personhood, a pivotal point of differentiation.
- Historical and societal factors, including the eastern invasion of the west in the 1960s (Transcendental Meditation) and a subsequent repackaging of this eastern invasion.
- Eastern meditation: a type of "high"?
- Relationship of *Christian* meditation to Christian prayer.
- Spiritual issues and concerns.

This is the journey of two different pathways. The journey involves science and spirituality, from brain imaging to the basic concepts of God. It also involves intrigue, controversy, and even adventure. So strap yourself into your seat and get ready to go. From the multiple convolutions of the brain, off into that place called the supernatural, here we go!

2 Mind and Body

So where do we start? Let's look at the following questions: In the general sense, is it good for one's health to meditate and/or pray? If so, is it good for the mind, the body, or both? Are there any potential unwanted side effects? Let's first look at eastern meditation in relating to these issues and then we'll consider Christian prayer.

Eastern Meditation: Health Benefits

The history of eastern meditation is primarily dated back to the formation of Hinduism. Hinduism was founded in India sometime between 1800 and 1000 B.C. It has no single documented founder but has many sects. In the Hindu belief system, God (Brahman) is an absolute spirit and everyone is a part of Brahman like "drops in the sea." Believers worship manifestations of Brahman (gods and goddesses). Reincarnation is an integral belief. Meditation can assist in releasing one from the cycles of reincarnation to achieve the final goal of union or absorption with Brahman.[1]

Buddhism was a later reformation of Hinduism. It traces its origin to the figure of Siddhartha Gautama (ca. 566–486 B.C.), the man who is revered in Buddhist tradition as the Buddha (in Sanskrit, Pali, "the Awakened One"). From its origin in northern India, the Buddhist tradition gradually expanded throughout the Indian subcontinent and much of the rest of Asia....In the last two centuries this Buddhist tradition has made its way to Europe and North America, making it one of the most widespread and influential of the world's religions.[2]

Buddhism teaches that meditation and the practice of good religious and moral behavior can lead to Nirvana, the state of enlightenment, although before achieving Nirvana, one is subject to repeated lifetimes that are good or bad depending on one's actions (karma).

The doctrines of Buddha describe temporal life as featuring "four noble truths": "existence is a realm of suffering; desire, along with the belief in the importance of one's self, causes suffering; achievement of Nirvana ends suffering; and Nirvana is attained only by meditation and by following the path of righteousness in action, thought and attitude." Buddhism was originally primarily an atheist religion but has developed in many places into a worship for its founder, Prince Siddhartha, known as Buddha.³

Buddhist meditation is defined as

the practice of mental concentration leading ultimately through a succession of stages to the final goal of spiritual freedom, nirvana. Meditation occupies a central place in Buddhism and combines, in its highest stages, the discipline of progressively increased introversion with the insight brought about by wisdom, or prajna.⁴

There are two aspects involved in Buddhist meditation. The first involves calming the mind (in Sanskrit, *samatha*), and the second involves using the calm mind to see reality clearly (in Sanskrit, *vipassana*). There is classically a willful or volitional clearing of all thoughts, feelings, and perceptions from the mind to achieve deeper awareness.

Recently, with the extensive emphasis on science within the west, there has been a refocusing on this ancient religion of Buddhism. A conference in Washington, D.C., featuring the Dalai Lama was called "Mind and Life XIII: Investigating the Mind. The Science and

Clinical Applications of Meditation." The Mind and Life Institute put on the program.[5] Brochures regarding the program stated the following: "The Mind and Life Institute is dedicated to creating a powerful working collaboration and research partnership between modern science and Buddhism—the world's two most powerful traditions for understanding the nature of reality and investigating the mind."

Although there is an increased emphasis on the science of eastern meditation within its traditional spiritual environment, there is also a movement to utilize this meditation style outside of its usual spiritual context. A review article from the *International Journal of Psychotherapy* concluded: "Meditation is an ancient technique that has recently been extracted from its spiritual framework, and applied to therapy for the enhancement of personal well-being."[6] It is within this context of personal well-being, of wellness, that a further increased emphasis is being seen not only in the scientific community but in the lay press as well.

The magazine *Real Simple* had an article on eastern meditation that opened as follows: "If meditation were a drug, its benefits would be almost too amazing for belief. Over the past decade, researchers have found that regular practice can lower blood pressure, decrease anxiety, improve immune function, increase vitality, and improve sleep."[7] The article went on to discuss further the health benefits of eastern meditation and then gave concrete examples of how to perform it and so forth.

A *Time* magazine cover article titled, "The Science of Meditation," indicated that 10 million American adults practice some form of meditation regularly, twice as many as a decade ago.[8] In the article, there was a section called "How to Meditate." It outlined the following four steps: (1) find a quiet place, (2) close your eyes, (3) pick a word, any word, and (4) say it again and again. It was also noted that one does not have to repetitively say a word over and over again. There may also be concentration on one's breathing, a ticking clock, and so forth.

Eastern meditation has been the subject of many studies. It achieved an increased prominence in the west partly due to Herbert Benson, a professor of medicine at Harvard Medical School, in his 1970s bestseller *The Relaxation Response*.[9] He measured meditators in his lab and found that the effects were essentially the opposite of the classic "fight or flight" response. Meditation decreased the heart rate, respiratory rate, blood pressure, oxygen consumption, and muscle tension. Further studies of meditating subjects have confirmed these decreases in blood pressure and heart rate as well as galvanic skin responses (skin electrical sensitivity).[10]

A study was presented at a recent American Heart Association meeting on the role of meditation in metabolic syndrome. Metabolic syndrome is noted to be a collection of conditions that can lead to heart disease, including high blood pressure and increased blood sugar levels. The study reported that meditation could reduce the severity of the risk factors in metabolic syndrome. A significant decrease in the levels of blood pressure and blood sugar was noted.[11]

Several other studies have shown that meditation and related practices cause changes in the brain's electrical activity.[12] Further research has also reported an improvement in immune function with meditation.[13]

A report to the Office on Alternative Medical Systems and Practices of the National Institutes of Health revealed a number of conclusions regarding meditation. Some of them follow:

1. Meditation reduces blood levels of cortisol, the stress hormone.
2. Meditation is associated with a longer life span, better quality of life, fewer hospitalizations, and reduced health care costs.
3. Regular meditation allays anxiety and reduces the severity of chronic pain.
4. Meditation can decrease blood cholesterol.
5. Meditation is a useful adjunct in controlling substance abuse.[14]

In summary, and although this is but a brief overview, we can see that there is documentation of a number of health benefits with eastern meditation.

Eastern meditation can result in the "relaxation response" (as noted previously), which has positive effects involving multiple bodily systems.

Eastern Meditation: Adverse Side Effects

There are also adverse or unwanted side effects of eastern meditation that are not as commonly known. These adverse consequences of eastern meditation are typically either physical or psychological in nature. One study looked at longtime meditators and found adverse side effects during or after meditation in 62.9 percent of subjects; 7.4 percent experienced profoundly adverse effects.[15] Side effects that were reported included relaxation-induced anxiety and panic (instead of a sense of relaxation there was a sense of anxiety or panic), paradoxical increases in tension (the opposite of the relaxation that was expected), boredom, pain, impaired reality testing (losing the sense of reality), confusion and disorientation, feeling spaced out, depression, increased negativity, being more judgmental, and feeling addicted to meditation. Other adverse effects that have been noted include uncomfortable kinesthetic (bodily) sensations, mild dissociation (a sense of being separated or disconnected), feelings of guilt, psychosis-like symptoms (delusions, hallucinations, loss of contact with reality), grandiosity, exaggerated sense of self-importance, elation, destructive behavior, and suicidal feelings.[16] A defenselessness has also been described, which in turn can produce fear, anger, apprehension, and despair.[17] These findings were all very similar to a large German study that was undertaken separately.[18] Another psychiatric side effect that has been noted is depersonalization. Depersonalization has been defined as a "sense of dreamlike unreality and a loss of the sense of one's own identity, often resulting from stress or anxiety."[19] A conclusion from one study on long-term meditation indicated that a depersonalized state could become an apparently permanent mode of functioning.[20]

There has been a relationship documented between eastern meditation and seizure-like activity. This is an association with enhanced complex partial epileptic-like signs, defined in the *Merck Manual* as staring, performing automatic purposeless movements, and uttering unintelligible sounds without understanding what is said, with subsequent residual mental confusion.[21] Meditators in this study displayed a significantly wider range of these complex partial epileptic-like signs. Experience of vibrations, hearing one's name called, paranormal phenomena, profound meaning from reading poetry/prose, and religious phenomenology were particularly frequent among meditators. The number of years practicing meditation was significantly correlated with the incidence of complex partial signs.[22]

So we can see that although there is documentation of a number of health benefits with eastern meditation, there are also adverse side effects or consequences. These side effects not only involve physical health concerns but psychological concerns as well.

Next, since we have only been looking at eastern meditation to this point, we'll examine Christian prayer. Let's look at some of the health benefits and documented adverse side effects involving Christian prayer.

Christian Prayer: Health Benefits

Christian prayer also has shown documented health benefits. Studies looking at Christian prayer have documented greater life satisfaction, less death anxiety, and lower rates of alcohol disorders among respondents who frequently read the Bible or prayed privately.[23]

When the studies are expanded to include church going and other religious activities there is even more information available. A major reason for this is that it is hard to separate the benefits of Christian prayer alone from the typical Christian lifestyle, which usually includes church-going activities with related social supports and so forth. Harold Koenig, M.D., discussed this in his book *Is Religion Good for Your Health? The Effects of Religion on Physical and Mental Health.*[24] He compiled the results of studies showing the benefits of either "devout religious commitment" (predominantly Christian religious commitment although some studies involved the Jewish religion) or "frequent involvement in both private and public religious activities" (predominantly Christian churches, although some studies included Jewish synagogues). In his conclusion, he divided these benefits into effects on mental health and physical health.

The benefits to mental health included a perceived improved ability to cope with stressful life circumstances, lower rates and improved recovery from depression, greater well-being and morale, higher self-esteem, an internal locus of control, marital adjustment and satisfaction, more rapid adaptation in caregivers of patients with dementia or end-stage cancer, lower rates of suicide, lower rates of anxiety disorder, lower rates of alcoholism and drug use, higher social support, happiness, adjustment, usefulness, higher life satisfaction, and as an advanced predictor of positive mood in young adults.

The benefits relating to physical health included improved functional ability at any given level of a chronic illness, lower levels of physical disability among older persons at one, two, and three years of follow-up, more rapid recovery from hip fracture, lower pain levels perceived by patients with end-stage cancer, lower rates of cigarette smoking, lower blood pressure (both systolic and diastolic), lower risk of stroke in controlled analyses, fewer myocardial infarctions (heart attacks), and a lower death rate from coronary artery disease and following cardiac surgery.[25]

As we have seen, there are health benefits noted with Christian prayer alone. Many more studies have shown health-related benefits with a typical Christian lifestyle (usually including church-going activities with related social supports, etc). These benefits involve both mental and physical health.

Next, since we have reviewed some of the health benefits of Christian prayer, let us now discuss some of the documented adverse side effects or consequences.

Christian Prayer: Adverse Side Effects

In compiling information regarding the adverse side effects of Christian prayer, I did a computer search as I had done with eastern meditation in obtaining the studies documented previously. This included conducting a search of *Pubmed* and *PsychINFO*. Unlike the studies involving eastern meditation, however, there was no information available regarding Christian prayer and adverse side effects.

Why is this? The best answer I found is from the *British Journal of Medical Psychology* in an article called "Why Do Psychiatrists Neglect Religion?" The bulk of the abstract from the article is as follows:

> The gap which exists between psychiatry and religion is a relatively recent phenomenon and is partly related to psychiatry's progress in elucidating the biological and psychological causes of mental illness, rendering religious explanations superfluous. In ad-

dition, it is often assumed that religious attitudes are inevitably linked with phenomena such as dependence and guilt which are frequently seen as undesirable. Psychiatrists and psychologists tend to be less religiously oriented than their patients, which may further increase the professional's idea that religious beliefs are associated with disturbance. However, it has long been suspected that a positive relation exists between religion and mental health, and recently, the psychology of religion has provided empirical support for this idea. Psychiatry faces the challenge to accommodate this evidence into theory and practice.[26]

Thus, we can see that there is a "gap" that has formed between psychiatry and religion. It is this "gap" that has likely contributed to the noted lack of information regarding Christian prayer and possible adverse side effects.

In summary, we have looked at the documented health benefits and adverse side effects of both eastern meditation and Christian prayer. This information is important background as we proceed in our assessment of the two. In the next chapter we will begin looking at basic differences involving the brain itself when one practices eastern meditation as opposed to Christian prayer.

3 The Meditation Model

In the 2001 book *Why God Won't Go Away: Brain Science and the Biology of Belief,* authors Andrew Newberg, M.D., and Eugene D'Aquili, M.D., Ph.D., discuss their research involving Tibetan meditators and Franciscan nuns.[27] Newberg is an assistant professor in the department of radiology in the division of nuclear medicine and an instructor in the department of religious studies at the University of Pennsylvania. D'Aquili was a clinical assistant professor in the Department of Psychiatry at the University of Pennsylvania for 12 years. These authors studied a series of Tibetan meditators and Franciscan nuns and assessed their individual brain changes during meditation. Each of the meditators was given a radioactive tracer that was injected through an intravenous line and recorded the brain blood flow changes both prior to and at the peak of meditation. A single photon emission computerized tomography (SPECT) scanner was utilized for assessing the brain blood flow changes. Those areas of the brain that are more active would thus show an increase in blood flow.

The meditators individually would sit in a quiet room with an intravenous line and a string attached to a finger. When each meditator would individually reach the peak of his or her meditation, he or she would pull on the string, thus alerting the researcher to inject the radioactive tracer and study the brain blood flow at the peak episode of meditation. In this way there could be a comparison of the brain before meditation and during the peak of meditation.

During the study, each Tibetan meditator would sit in the quiet area in a position of comfort, with pillows available, such as in the lotus position with legs crossed. Incense was allowed throughout the study. The focus would be on a gradual calming of the conscious mind. The journey was noted to be into an inner, deeper reality. One of the meditators described it as feeling "timeless and infinite," "a part of every one and everything in existence." When the peak of the meditation was reached, the meditator would pull on the string thereby alerting the researchers to inject the radioactive tracer and study the brain blood flow at this peak episode of meditation.

Likewise, each Franciscan nun would sit in the quiet area with the intravenous line and a string attached to her finger. She would perform a verbal practice, which the authors called "centering prayer," defined as follows: "Centering prayer requires the individual to focus attention on a phrase from the Bible or prayer, over a period of time, with the goal of 'opening themselves to being in the presence of God.'" Each nun would thus meditate on a phrase from the Bible or Christian prayer. At the point when she would feel the strongest sense of God's presence, she would likewise pull the string.

These studies are part of the ongoing research to help explain what happens during these mystical states. A model of religious and mystical states was first introduced by the above-noted authors in 1993 (*Zygon* 28: 177–200), with further elaboration in 1999.[28] Within this meditation model, there are two broad categories of meditation: passive approaches and active approaches.

Passive approaches are defined as meditative techniques "in which the intention is to clear the mind of all conscious thought." Active approaches are defined as meditative techniques "in which the goal is to focus the mind completely on some object of attention—a mantra for example, or some symbol or scriptural verse." The passive approach attempts to clear the mind of any outside perceptions or interruptions to seek a deeper inner awareness. The active approach attempts to focus solely on an outside object, symbol, or phrase with the goal of clearing the mind of any thoughts not directed at this specific outside object, symbol, or phrase. The passive meditation approach is practiced by many Buddhist orders, and I am thus going to categorize it for the purposes of this book under the term "eastern passive meditation." Christian meditation, however, would be subcategorized as one of the active approaches of meditation. The Christian meditator would actively focus on some outside object pertaining to Christianity (i.e., a Bible verse, a cross, etc.). For the purposes of this book, I will thus use the term "Christian active meditation." Let's look at these two broad categories of meditation in more detail to better understand them.

Eastern Passive Meditation

The passive meditation approach is practiced by many Buddhist orders. As noted in chapter two, the intention is to clear all thoughts, emotions, and perceptions from the mind to achieve deeper awareness. When the meditator begins to concentrate or focus on meditating, the brain attention association area (attention area) increases or lights up. This attention area is located near the front of the brain in the right prefrontal cortex. In the process of trying to clear the mind of any extraneous thoughts, there is a calming down of two other areas further back in the brain. These areas are called the orientation association areas (orientation areas) located in the posterior portion of the parietal lobes. Quoting Newberg and D'Aquili:

> The left orientation area is responsible for creating the mental sensation of a limited physically defined body, while the right orientation area is associated with generating the sense of spatial coordinates that provides the matrix in which the body can be oriented. In simpler terms the left orientation area

creates the brain's spatial sense of self, while the right side creates the physical space in which that self can exist.[29]

The meditator thus uses the attention area in focusing on calming down the brain and quieting these orientation areas. A brain circuit is set up involving the deeper brain structures, including the thalamus (an important relay station with many interconnecting brain pathways) and the hippocampus (located at the base of both temporal lobes, thought to play a role in memory). Using this brain circuitry, there is a gradual dampening of the input to the orientation areas. As the meditator continues to try to clear the mind of all thoughts, a further decrease in the flow to these orientation areas occurs. At the peak of meditation, both orientation areas go dark. There is believed to be a complete shutdown of any input to the orientation areas. Without any input, the left orientation area would not be able to find its sense of self—its self would, in essence, become limitless. Likewise, the right orientation area would not be able to find its sense of space—it would, therefore, become spaceless or convey a sense of the infinite. The meditator thus experiences the limitlessness or sense of the infinite, which is so common with eastern meditation.

Christian Active Meditation

Within this model, the Christian meditator will also begin by concentrating or focusing. With this attention or concentration beginning the meditation process, there is a lighting up, or increase of the attention area located in the right frontal cortex. This attention area, however, is not focusing on calming down the orientation areas as in the previous eastern passive meditation approach. Instead, the attention is focused on a Biblical phrase or a Christian prayer.

For the purposes of this discussion, let's say that the focus is on an image of Jesus. The attention area, by focusing on an image of Jesus, will encourage increased activity to the right orientation area. Again, the right orientation area is associated with the brain's sense of space, whereas the left orientation area is associated with the brain's sense of self. A different brain circuit is set up, again involving the deeper brain structures including the thalamus and hippocampus, gradually facilitating the input to the right orientation area. As the attention area focuses more and more on the image of Jesus, there is a decrease in any input not involving this contemplation.

With the attention area focusing strongly on this image, there is an increase in the blood flow to the right orientation area and a decrease in the blood flow to the left orientation area. The right orientation area, which creates the sense of physical space, receives this increased focus on Jesus, since no other input is being allowed through the attention area. The left orientation area, which creates the brain's sense of self, decreases. Therefore, at the peak of meditation, the left orientation area decreases and there is a feeling of unity or joining of the self together with Jesus. At the peak of the meditation, there is a darkening of the left orientation area with the maximal blood flow of the right orientation area. Thus, there would be an experience of the personal sense of oneness or union with Jesus, which has been described in Christian meditation.

4 Crossing the Bridge

In the previous chapter we introduced a scientific model of meditation in furthering our contrast involving Christian prayer with eastern meditation. However, since this book involves spirituality as well as science, we need to look at the spiritual dimension also. This chapter includes pertinent spiritual concepts as important background before we get back to the meditation model. Let's start with a discussion regarding Christianity, and then we will proceed with eastern religious beliefs.

In looking initially at the beliefs of Christianity, we must first look at this person of Jesus Christ. What did he claim? Obviously, a thorough discourse is well beyond the confines of this book. Nevertheless, a few major points are helpful for the purposes of our discussion.

Jesus Claimed to Be the Son of God

Who did Jesus Christ say he was? He claimed to be God's son. Some Bible verses in which he made this claim include:

Matthew 16:15-17: "He said to them 'but who do you say that I am?' Simon Peter replied, 'You are the Christ, the Son of the living God.' And Jesus answered him, 'Blessed are you, Simon Barjona, for flesh and blood has not revealed this to you, but my Father who is in heaven.'"[30]

Mark 14:61-62: "But he was silent and made no answer. Again the high priest asked him, 'Are you the Christ, the Son of the Blessed?' And Jesus said, 'I am; and you will see the Son of man sitting at the right hand of Power, and coming with the clouds of heaven.'"

Jesus Claimed to Be Equal to God the Father

Who else did Jesus claim to be? He claimed to be equal with God the Father. Some Bible verses in which he claimed this include:

John 5:18: "…he not only broke the Sabbath, but also called God his Father, making himself equal with God."

John 8:19: "They said to him therefore, 'where is your Father?' Jesus answered, 'you know neither me nor my Father; if you knew me, you would know my Father also.'"

John 10:30: "I and the Father are one."

John 5:21-23: "For as the Father raises the dead and gives them life, so also the Son gives life to whom he will. The Father judges no one, but has given all judgement to the Son, that all may honor the Son, even as they honor the Father. He who does not honor the Son does not honor the Father who sent him."

Jesus Claimed to Be The Way, The Truth, and The Life

What is another claim that Jesus made? He claimed to be the way, the truth, and the life. Bible verses include:

John 14:6: "Jesus said to him, 'I am the way, and the truth, and the life. No one comes to the Father, but by me. If you had known me, you would have known my Father also'…"

John 8:31–32: "Jesus then said to Jews who had believed in him, 'If you continue in my word, you are truly my disciples, and you will know the truth, and the truth will make you free.'"

John 18:37: "Jesus answered [to Pontius Pilate], 'You say that I am a king. For this I was born, and for this I have come into the world, to bear witness to the truth. Every one who is of the truth hears my voice.'"

John 20:30–31: "Now Jesus did many other signs in the presence of the disciples, which are not written in this book; but these are written that you may believe that Jesus is the Christ, the Son of God, and that in believing you may have life in his name."

So who did Jesus Christ say he was? He claimed to be the son of God, he claimed to be equal with God the Father, and he claimed to be the way, the truth, and the life. These claims end up being a big stumbling block within Christianity that differs from the eastern religions.

Based on the subject matter of this book, contrasting Christian prayer with eastern meditation, it's important that we discuss these differences between Christianity and the major eastern religions further. In this chapter, I would like to concentrate on Buddhism rather than Hinduism in this contrast. The reasons are fourfold:

1. Buddhism has a clearly defined founder, which simplifies things.
2. The Tibetan branch of Buddhism has a living recognized leader (the Dalai Lama), which further simplifies things.
3. Buddhism is actively involved in scientific research regarding the field of neurotheology (see the conferences organized by the Mind and Life Institute, as noted in chapter two).
4. Certain Buddhist documents and readings I reviewed in preparation for this book were felt to be directly applicable to our following discussion. Nevertheless, many of the points that are developed could be applicable to Hinduism as well.

We have looked at three basic claims of Christianity. Now let's examine three basic claims of Buddhism.

The Buddha Has Revealed the Truth

Trust in truth, you who love the truth, for the kingdom of righteousness is founded upon earth. The darkness of error is dispelled by the light of truth.

We can see our way and take firm and certain steps. The Buddha, our Lord, has revealed the truth. The truth cures our diseases and redeems us from perdition; the truth strengthens us in life and in death; the truth alone can conquer the evils of error. Rejoice at the glad tidings![31]

Seek Not Self but Seek the Truth

Learn to distinguish between self and truth. Self is the cause of selfishness and the source of evil; truth cleaves to no self; it is universal and leads to justice and righteousness. Self, that which seems to those who love their self as their being, is not the eternal, the everlasting, the imperishable. Seek not self, but seek the truth.

If we liberate our souls from our petty selves, wish no ill to others, and become clear as a crystal diamond reflecting the light of truth, what a radiant picture will appear in us mirroring things as they are, without the admixture of burning desires, without the distortion of erroneous illusion, without the agitation of clinging and unrest...

Let us take our refuge in the Buddha, for he has found the everlasting in the transient. Let us take our refuge in that which is the immutable in the changes of existence. Let us take our refuge in the truth that is established through the enlightenment of the Buddha. Let us take our refuge in the community of those who seek the truth and endeavor to live in the truth.[32]

Nirvana, the State of Enlightenment

This truly, is the Peace; this is the Highest, namely the end of all formations, the forsaking of every substratum of rebirth, the fading away of craving: detachment, extinction—Nirvana…

The extinction of greed, the extinction of anger, and the extinction of delusion: this indeed, is called Nirvana.[33]

From the above we can note the Buddhist claims that "Buddha, our Lord, has revealed the truth" and to "seek not self—but seek the truth." This is in conflict with the teachings of Jesus who claimed that he is "the way, the truth, and the life." So, what do we make of this? Both Christianity and Buddhism claim to be the truth. Can they both reveal the same truth? What is the truth? Obviously, both have some elements of truth within them. One similar belief of the two religions would include the foregoing of some lower basic physical desires in the search for a higher spiritual good. Another is the noted wishing of no ill will toward others. But overall, does this truth really exist? And if so, what is it in relation to either Christianity and/or Buddhism?

In addressing these questions, a quote from a Buddhist source offers some interesting insights. In the preface of *Buddha, The Gospel* the following is noted:

> It is a remarkable fact that the two greatest religions of the world, Christianity and Buddhism, present so many striking coincidences in the philosophical basis as well as in the ethical applications of their faith, while their modes of systematizing them in dogmas are radically different; and it is difficult to understand why these agreements should have caused animosity, instead of creating sentiments of friendship and good-will....[34]

The author continues:

> The main trouble arises from a wrong conception of Christianity. There are many Christians who assume that Christianity alone is in possession of truth and that man could not, in the natural way of his moral evolution, have obtained that nobler conception of life, which enjoins the practice of a universal

good will towards both friends and enemies. This narrow view of Christianity is refuted by the mere existence of Buddhism.

Must we add that the lamentable exclusiveness that prevails in many Christian churches is not based upon Scriptural teachings, but upon a wrong metaphysics? All the essential moral truths of Christianity, especially the principle of a universal love, of the eradication of hatred, are in our opinion deeply rooted in the nature of things, and do not, as is often assumed, stand in contradiction to the cosmic order of the world…

From this Buddhist perspective, therefore, the "exclusiveness" of Christianity—the "wrong conception"—appears to be the problem. This is the Christian belief that Christianity, alone, is in possession of the truth. It obviously excludes Buddhism, as well as other religions, resulting in "animosity, instead of creating sentiments of friendship and good will." Buddhism certainly appears more "inclusive." Why can't Christianity be more inclusive and contribute to this "friendship and good will"? What is it about Christianity that has resulted in its history of "exclusiveness"?

To answer this question regarding the exclusiveness that Christianity has historically portrayed, let's look at the Old Testament. We need to look at the foundations that were laid down by the God in the Old Testament. We need to look at the covenant He set up with His chosen people.

At the time of the flood, God established his covenant with Noah: "But I will establish my covenant with you; and you shall come into the ark, you, your sons, your wife, and your sons' wives with you" (Genesis 6:18). He later told Abraham in Genesis 15:5–6: "And he brought him outside and said, 'Look toward heaven and number the stars, if you are able to number them.' Then he said to him, 'So shall your descendants be.' And he believed the Lord; and he reckoned it to him as righteousness." There was further confirmation of this covenant to Jacob in his dream (Genesis 28:13–15). But we really see the covenant defined through Moses in Exodus chapters 19 through 24. He gives Moses the Ten Commandments, with the most important for our discussion being the one given the top priority, the First Commandment: "I am the Lord your God, who brought you out of the land of Egypt, out of the house of bondage. You shall have no other gods before me" (Exodus 20:2–3).

God further indicates to Moses that the Israelite nation is a special people, a chosen, exclusive people: "Behold, I make a covenant. Before all your people I will do marvels, such as have not been wrought in all the earth or in any nation; and all the people among whom you are shall see the work of the Lord; for it is a terrible thing that I will do with you…" (Exodus 34:10).

Moses had to put up with frequent threats of revolt, murmurings against himself and against God, dealings with idol worship (Exodus 32: the golden calf), open rebellion (Numbers 16), and ended up spending an extra 40 years with the people wandering the desert because of lack of belief (Numbers 14:34). The Israelites were noted to be a "stiff-necked people" (Deuteronomy 9:6). Because of all this, Moses gives a sermon to the Israelites in Deuteronomy as they are finally ready to enter the Promised Land. The exclusiveness of the Israelites as the chosen people is again reiterated: "For you are a people Holy to the Lord your God; the Lord your God has chosen you to be a people for His own possession, out of all the peoples that are on the face of the earth" (Deuteronomy 7:6).

In Deuteronomy 10:14–15, Moses tells the Israelites: "Behold, to the Lord your God belong heaven and the heaven of heavens, earth with all that is in it; yet the Lord set his heart in love upon your fathers and chose their descendants after them, you above all peoples, as at this day." The emphasis of God as the most important is noted again in Deuteronomy 6:4–9:

> Hear, O Israel: The Lord our God is one Lord; and you shall love the Lord your God with all your heart, and with all your soul, and with all your might. And these words which I command you this day shall be upon your heart; and you shall teach them diligently to your children, and shall talk of them when you

> sit in your house, and when you walk by the way, and when you lie down, and when you rise. And you shall bind them as a sign upon your hand, and they shall be as frontlets between your eyes. And you shall write them on the doorposts of your house and on your gates.

Thus, in Deuteronomy Moses repeats to the people that their God is the only God, that they must honor Him, and that they are specially chosen. The exclusiveness of Christianity begins with the exclusive relationship defined between the God of the Old Testament and the Israelite people. To recognize the coexistence of another deity, another belief system or ultimate "truth" (i.e., Buddhism, etc.) would go against this constantly repeated theme of the God of the Old Testament. This God of the Old Testament reiterates that he is the only God, with His commandments (not suggestions) to follow.

Within this context, therefore, where would the Buddhist religion fit in? We can gain some insight into this answer by looking closely at Deuteronomy 4:15–20 (emphasis mine):

> And beware lest you act corruptly by making a graven image for yourselves, in the form of any figure, the likeness of male or female, the likeness of any beast that is on the earth, the likeness of any

winged bird that flies in the air, the likeness of anything that creeps on the ground, the likeness of any fish that is in the water under the earth. And beware lest you lift up your eyes to heaven, and when you see the sun and the moon and the stars, all the host of heaven, you will be drawn away and worship them and serve them, *things which the Lord your God has allotted to all the peoples under the whole heaven.* But the Lord has taken you, and brought you forth out of the iron furnace, out of Egypt, to be a people of his own possession, as at this day.

We can infer from this verse that while the Israelites are the specially chosen people, God has allotted to all the other peoples on earth a less direct involvement, including the ways of the sun, the moon, the stars, and so forth.... With the Israelites, He has specially chosen them and has formed an actual covenant with them. Yet he has not totally abandoned all other peoples as they can still gain insights into Him through the physical workings of nature. A certain, incomplete knowledge of God can thus be made by a careful observance of the laws of nature, which God has created. One can learn something about God by carefully watching what has been made.

With the above in mind, it is interesting to look at another quote from the preface of *Buddha, The Gospel*:

"Now Buddhism is a religion which knows of no supernatural revelation, and proclaims doctrines that require no other argument than the 'come and see.' The Buddha bases his religion solely upon man's knowledge of the nature of things, upon provable truth."[35]

Buddhism could thus be considered an almost expected development among a people who did not have the more direct involvement and chosen relationship with God. Remember that the Buddha lived approximately 500 years before the birth of Christ. This certainly would help explain the truths that are seen within Buddhism as they could be gleaned from the natural laws of the creator. Yet without the special relationship, the supernatural revelation, and the covenant, the truths are left incomplete, they fall short. They are truths, but they are not the fullness of the truth. For God is greater than what exists in nature.

But the story doesn't end here. In Deuteronomy we also see the fatherhood of God described by Moses: "You are the sons of the Lord your God..." (Deuteronomy 14:1). And also "Know then in your heart that, as a man disciplines his son, the Lord your God disciplines you" (Deuteronomy 8:5). It is a part of Christian belief that within this spirit of fatherhood the God of the Old Testament sent his own son, who claimed to be one with Him. We can frequently see in the New Testament that Jesus claims to do nothing of his own accord. Everything is done with the authority of the Father. "When you have lifted up the Son of man, then you will know that I am he, and that I do nothing on my own authority but speak thus as the Father taught me. And he who sent me is with me; he has not left me alone, for I always do what is pleasing to him" (John 8:28–29).

There is the public expression of Jesus as God's son in Matthew 3:16–17, with the baptizing by John the Baptist: "And when Jesus was baptized, he went up immediately from the water and behold, the heavens were opened and he saw the Spirit of God descending like a dove, and alighting on him; and lo, a voice from heaven, saying: 'this is my beloved Son, with whom I am well pleased.'" We see this similarly when his close apostles saw his radiance as he talked with Moses and Elijah. Again, a voice was heard from above exclaiming, "This is my beloved Son, with whom I am well pleased; listen to him" (Matthew 17:1–5).

The exclusiveness of having one God, the Father, is a consistent teaching of Christ. The exclusiveness of having only one people—the chosen people—however, is not. This is where Jesus changes the exclusiveness of the chosen people to the inclusiveness of all people through him. Simeon foretold this at the presentation of the baby Jesus at the temple: "…a light for revelation to the Gentiles, and for glory to thy people Israel" (Luke 2:32). It was fulfilled through Jesus, the mediator of a new covenant (Hebrews 12:24), the new covenant in his blood (Luke 22:20). Jesus opened up this fatherhood of God, this supernatural relationship to all people. "For God so loved the world that he gave

37

his only Son, that whoever believes in him should not perish but have eternal life" (John 3:16).

The exclusiveness of the God of the Old Testament remains, but the inclusiveness of all people is fulfilled through Jesus Christ. Instead of creating mere "sentiments of friendship and good will" (as mentioned in the *Buddha, The Gospel* passage above), it is the Christian belief that through his passion, death, and resurrection Christ brings the language of love, the pathway to the fullness of truth. And he exhorts his followers to bring this "good news" to others.

> All authority in heaven and on earth has been given to me. Go therefore and make disciples of all nations, baptizing them in the name of the Father and of the Son and of the Holy Spirit, teaching them to observe all that I have commanded you; and lo, I am with you always, to the close of the age (Matthew 12:18–20).

It comes down to the point where a choice must be made. The God of the Old Testament claimed to be the one true God and commanded to be followed as such. Jesus claimed to be the son of God, equal to God the Father, and "the way, the truth and the life." The choice has to be made either to follow Jesus or not to follow him.

For the purposes of this book, let's assume Jesus is right and that he is who he said he was. This would require the gift of faith in making this assumption. But again, for the purposes of this book, let's take that bridge of faith across any abyss of doubt. Once taking that bridge of faith, we can turn around on the other side of the bridge and look back at this issue of Christian prayer and eastern meditation. Let's get back to the meditation model that we've previously discussed. We can begin by first assessing the meditation model further from a Christian perspective.

5 On the Other Side

In viewing the meditation model from a Christian perspective, I would like to look specifically at the meditation model and the person of Jesus Christ. I would like to discuss what we now know about meditation and the theoretical model previously presented in conjunction with what we know from the Christian gospels about the person of Jesus Christ. This will also prompt some thoughts about Christian prayer and Christian meditation as a whole.

The Meditation Model and the Person of Jesus Christ

One of the things Jesus did multiple times in the gospels was pray, frequently going off to a quiet, solitary place. For instance, in Luke 5:16: "But he would withdraw to deserted places to pray." Mark 1:35: "Rising very early before dawn, he left and went off to a deserted place, where he prayed." Luke 6:12: "In those days, he departed to the mountain to pray, and he spent the night in prayer to God."

He taught his followers to pray, both in example (as above) and by explanation. In Luke 11:1 he taught the disciples "The Lord's Prayer." In Luke 18:1 he told his disciples a parable to show them that they should always pray and not give up.

If we were to extrapolate the findings of the current meditation model onto what we know about Jesus, it would be reasonable to conclude that Jesus was an active meditator. His prayers were active and directed to the Father. His prayers were purposeful and for guidance. And his prayers were personal.

Going off to solitary places would have allowed him to increase his concentration. Without interruptions, alone, in quiet contemplation we can imagine his thoughts focusing more and more on heaven. It's conceivable that the findings in Christ's brain would have been similar to the active meditation model, which we discussed in chapter three. The attention area of Christ's brain, by focusing on God in heaven, would encourage increased activity to the right orientation area. Again, the right orientation area is associated with the brain's sense of space, whereas the left orientation area is associated with the brain's sense of self. As the attention area focuses more and more on God in heaven, there is an increase in the blood flow to the right orientation area and a decrease in the blood flow to the left orientation area. At the peak of meditation, there is a darkening of the left orientation area with the maximal blood flow of the right orientation area. This could be interpreted as a feeling of unity or the joining to-

41

gether of Jesus' individual sense of self with God in heaven.

But this is beyond mere meditation. He is not just thinking or contemplating about God or heaven but is actually communicating with the Father. It is at this point that we have to believe Jesus is actually praying. He is in actual contact with God, the Father. This is a key to Christian prayer. It is active, personal, and communicative.

Christian Meditation: An Active Process

From the above we can further propose that Christian meditation, like Christian prayer, is an active process. With Christian meditation, however, there is contemplation without the personal communication associated with prayer. I would define Christian meditation for our purposes as a contemplation of the mysteries of God as illuminated by the truths within the Christian faith. Spiritual growth can come from the internal cognitive processing of the contemplation within the light of faith. It is also from this Christian meditative process, however, that the thought development can ascend upward. Christian meditation can thus be a springboard from which prayer, the actual personal communication with God, develops. To summarize then, Christian meditation is an active process that can result in spiritual growth in and of itself or as the beginning of a transition into Christian prayer.

6 Personhood—A Key Difference

What is personhood? Let's simply define it for our purposes as an individual's sense of self, of uniqueness. So what does this issue of personhood have to do with our ongoing contrast between Christian prayer and eastern meditation? As we shall see, it is an important concept and defines one of the key differences between the two approaches.

Christian prayer itself involves a personal relationship with God; the sense of person or personhood is maintained by the one praying. The uniqueness and individuality of the person praying remains intact during the prayer, as does the personal nature of God. This personhood remains distinct and intact even after death, within the Christian concept of the afterlife.

This is not the case with the classic eastern theology of pantheism, however. God is in everything: water, sand, trees, etc. But the personhood of each individual is not included in the end. The uniqueness, the individuality of each person, ends up being only transitory. I would partially relate this to the eastern concept of reincarnation. How can the personhood of each individual remain within the ongoing cycle of death and rebirth as someone or something else? The Buddha himself was noted to have more than 100,000 previous lives.[36] Nirvana could even be seen as a release (and a relief) from the ongoing wheel of existence but at the cost of one's individuality.

Let's review another quote from *Buddha, The Gospel* to expand on this. I have italicized two specific phrases in this quotation for emphasis:

> All compound things shall be dissolved again, worlds will break to pieces and *our individualities will be scattered*; but the words of Buddha will remain forever. The extinction of self is salvation; the annihilation of self is the condition of enlightenment; *the blotting out of self* is Nirvana.[37]

If we revert to the meditation model from chapter three, we can discuss this issue of personhood further. Within the meditation model we noted that at the peak of eastern meditation both orientation areas of the brain go dark. This includes the left orientation area, which provides the sense of self, and the right orientation area, which provides the sense of space. During this peak of eastern meditation, the left orientation area is not able to find its sense of self—its self would in essence become limitless. Likewise, the right orientation area is not able to find its sense of space—it would, in essence, become spaceless or convey a sense of the infinite. Without the sense of self and devoid of the sense of space, how does one maintain personhood? One could consider it a pursuit in the act of becoming nothing, a nonperson to join the void.

It is this issue of personhood that I feel troubles most westerners regarding this eastern emphasis. It just doesn't feel "right." Why? Because there is such a premium placed on individuality and uniqueness in the west. To give this all up is contrary to the way most westerners think. And with Christianity, as we have noted, this sense of retained personhood, this unique ongoing personal relationship with God, is one of its core teachings.

7 The Eastern Invasion of the West

When did eastern meditation and the eastern influence become so popular in the west? What events brought this about, especially in the United States? And how do we relate those events to today and to our ongoing contrast involving Christian prayer and eastern meditation?

To begin this chapter, we must go back to the decade of the 1960s. Ah...yes...the sixties, that tumultuous decade that shook the American populace. Flashbacks include the hippie movement, the sexual revolution, "make love not war," the drug culture with LSD ("acid trips") and marijuana ("Mary Jane" or "weed"), bellbottom pants, Afros, Bob Dylan protest songs, "the generation gap," and Woodstock. It was in this environment that the story begins, with the start of the Transcendental Meditation movement.

The Transcendental Meditation movement was originally founded in India by Maharishi Mahesh Yogi in 1957.[38] Born Mehesh Prasad Varma, he attained a degree in physics from Ahallabad University in 1940.

Instead of pursuing science, however, he enrolled in a monastery in India and studied under a swami known as Guru Dev. After Guru Dev's death, Varma emerged from a period of seclusion and began teaching worldwide the movement of Transcendental Meditation. It was through these travels that the movement was first introduced to the west and eventually the United States.

What the Transcendental Meditation (TM) program offered was a system consisting of a daily meditation using a mantra (a word that is said over and over again to oneself). The Maharishi advocated giving a single mantra to each student at a short private ceremony.

With the Maharishi's background in physics, a key to the success of the movement in the west was the scientific substantiation of the meditation as a method of relaxation. A number of articles published in scientific journals at the time supported this and contributed to the movement's momentum. It was in 1967, however, that a blockbuster event occurred, propelling the movement to its peak. The enormously popular rock group, The Beatles, became followers of the Maharishi and endorsed TM. George Harrison learned of the Maharishi's presence in London and persuaded the other Beatles to attend the Maharishi's center in India .[39] This sole event contributed immensely to the movement's growth in the United States and Europe during the late 1960s and early 1970s. Nearly 1 million people were noted to have taken the basic TM course during this period. TM began to be taught in a variety of institutions supported by public funds, including U.S.

public schools. Government grants were obtained, supported by scientific documentation of the effects of the technique.

The movement was going so well that in 1972 the Maharishi announced the World Plan Executive Council. The goal of this council is the sharing of the Science of Creative Intelligence, which is the movement's comprehensive understanding of life and knowledge, to the whole world. Within this understanding, TM is noted to be the practical aspect. The Council has made many claims for the effects of the practice of TM, and their findings have been published in a variety of scientific journals. TM has been reported to improve not only individual mental, physical, and psychological health, but also to produce benefits in every sphere of life: individual, governmental, educational, social, environmental, economic, and spiritual.

The Maharishi and TM enjoyed tremendous success and became a household word in the United States in the early 1970s. They also brought considerable controversy and criticism. Others began challenging the findings of the TM movement. Questions regarding study designs, experimental controls, and the arrival at conclusions started to surface. The movement's reputation began to suffer. Documentation of psychiatric problems being precipitated by the practice of TM was released.[40] Interest began to wane. By 1976 the number of new people taking the introductory TM course declined considerably.

It was then that the movement instituted a new tact, that of levitation. A news article from the *Washington Post* (1977) is quite interesting.[41] The following are excerpts:

> The Transcendental Meditation movement of Maharishi Mahesh Yogi, which gained a measure of respectability and a host of government grants by scientifically documenting the effects of the technique, is now into levitation and disappearing. The hardcore disciples of the Maharishi—who attracted nearly a million people to their classes on meditation over the past two years—are now speaking excitedly of "supernormal" powers like levitation (lifting one's body into the air), "dematerializing yourself" and even flying through the air "like Peter Pan"...

The article continues:

> The new turn in the multi-million dollar a year TM movement comes at a time when the number of new people learning the age-old technique in official TM classes has dropped dramatically from a monthly peak of more than 40,000 people in this country less than two years ago, to no more than about 10,000 today.

The article indicated that a minimum donation of $1,000 would be needed for consideration in a demonstration.

Scientists have since scoffed at this proposal of levitation introduced by the TM proponents. An excerpt from the affidavit of a consultant to the Committee for the Scientific Investigation of Claims of the Paranormal follows:

> Many of the claims issued by the TM organization in their news releases and recruitment campaigns are not just badly mistaken and ill-conceived; they are worse. No competent scientist, on the basis of present scientific understanding, could seriously subscribe to the TM views. Mass meditation cannot be used to lessen the force of gravity...[42]

The *Skeptical Enquirer* magazine contained the following excerpt regarding levitation:

> Photographs distributed by TM officials showed devotees in a lotus position and seemingly floating in midair. The photos are misleading. No TM-er has yet demonstrated levitation to an outsider. The best they can show is the ability to flex one's legs while in a lotus position on a springy mattress and hop upward a short distance. The phony photos were

snapped when the supposed floater was at the top of a bounce.[43]

Various criticisms and controversies led to court cases involving the TM movement. In 1978 a significant legal blow occurred. The federal court in New Jersey ruled that TM was a religious practice. Based on this ruling, it could no longer be taught in the public schools, thus resulting in a further decrease of potential followers. In 1986 a civil lawsuit resulted in a significant jury award to pay for the psychiatric treatment of a former upper-level member of the movement. Accusations during the trial included the "deliberate pattern of fraud, deceit and misrepresentation" of those involved with the movement.[44] The jury found that the TM movement "defrauded him [the former member] with false promises of mental bliss and neglected to warn him about the possibility of adverse side effects."[45]

A former chairman of the physics department at the Maharishi International University (now the Maharishi University of Management, Fairfield, Iowa) has since come out strongly against the TM movement in general and especially the scientific methodology utilized. He has been quoted as follows: "Because of the strong authoritarian (essentially cultic) aspects of the movement, only results supporting ideas generated by the movement leadership could receive any hearing. The 'scientific research' is without objectivity and is at times simply untrue."[46]

Although the movement exists to this day, it has since been included in the *Encyclopedic Handbook of Cults in America*.

So what happened? In retrospect, it would appear that the great respect for science in the west initially paved the pathway for TM. An excerpt from the *Encyclopedic Handbook of Cults in America* is enlightening:

> Finally, TM critics have charged the movement with an element of deception. They claim (with good evidence) that Maharishi brought TM to America but soon he discovered that it did not appeal to the masses he hoped to reach. Therefore, he created a new image, in part based upon the early scientific papers, and began to deny the religious elements…[47]

In other words, the focus was taken away from the eastern religious components and placed instead on the scientific. In the west we often look to science to better understand our world and to help us figure out our problems and difficulties. When there is scientific support for a concept or idea, it significantly adds to the respect it is given. The early scientific studies involving the relaxation effects of TM have been repetitively verified (even by those outside the TM movement) and provided a basis from which the movement made other, increasingly controversial claims. Mirroring its meteoric rise in the United Stated in the late 1960s was its fast descent in the mid 1970s as the controversy regarding these other claims increased. Nevertheless, new ground had been broken. The focus on scientific testing involving something like meditation was intriguing. And as a result of TM, eastern meditation was no longer so "foreign" in the west. The door was opened, and the eastern invasion came flooding in. The TM movement established eastern meditation as a part of the western world.

In the next chapter we'll relate these events involving TM to the current era and return to our ongoing contrast between Christian prayer and eastern meditation.

8 The Eastern Invasion Repackaged

What is the current status of eastern meditation in the west with the decline in popularity of TM? And what does this have to do with our contrast involving Christian prayer?

In addressing these questions I would like to offer the following proposal: Although TM is still practiced (on a considerably smaller scale) in the west, the main emphasis regarding eastern meditation has been to spin off in different directions away from TM. The reason for this spinoff is largely because of the tainted reputation of the TM movement itself. The eastern meditation momentum that was started with the TM movement is, therefore, continued without the excess "baggage." The first spinoff away from TM that we will discuss is a traditional eastern religious emphasis. A second spinoff is a nonreligious eastern meditation emphasis. These will both be discussed in further detail below. (Note: The New Age movement is another potential emphasis involving eastern meditation that will not be discussed.)

Traditional Eastern Religion Emphasis

The first option has been for the west to embrace the traditional eastern religion component from which eastern meditation originally came (i.e., the practice of Hinduism and/or Buddhism). This eliminates the controversy that has plagued the TM movement regarding whether it is a religion or not (the movement claiming it is not but the court ruling that it is, with its subsequent listing in the handbook of cults as noted in the previous chapter). This emphasis on returning to the traditional eastern religions thus takes TM totally out of the picture. The use of the language of Sanskrit or other traditional mantras is utilized with the eastern theological emphasis fully recognized and enhanced.

As previously noted, there has been a more recent movement to involve scientific study to further support and encourage the practice of eastern religion. This would include the research conferences involving Buddhism by the Mind and Life Institute that was discussed in chapter two. The gains made by the TM movement with respect to the initial scientific support of eastern meditation can, therefore, be carried forward within a traditional eastern religious setting. This focus on science appeals to the western mind-set and can further the growth, this time of the traditional eastern religion. At last count Buddhism (as our example) was listed as the world's fifth largest religion with 360 million followers. Among the 5 million Buddhists in United States, 1 million are western converts.[48]

Nonreligious Eastern Meditation Emphasis

Conversion to an eastern religion as noted previously can be difficult for many westerners, even with the scientific focus that is expounded at the conferences as discussed. Consequently, we see another choice, a different spinoff of the TM movement that is more in line with the ways of the west. Instead of fully embracing the eastern religion emphasis, as is done above, this choice does the opposite. There is a total de-emphasis on the eastern religion component. The TM movement attempted—and still attempts—to deny any religious component even though this has been ruled otherwise. With a nonreligious eastern meditation emphasis, however, there is no longer focus on eastern religion. This is simply eastern meditation without the eastern religion, or what is called "nonreligious" meditation (quotes for emphasis are mine). There is no longer the issue of the lack of familiarity of most westerners with eastern religions. Yet the scientific emphasis regarding this kind of meditation continues. This nonreligious meditation is the kind of meditation that fills so many self-help books and magazines today. It is the current "rage" in the search for stress management, improvement in self-control, self-actualization, and so forth.

For example, we noted the four steps in chapter two including:

1. Find a quiet place.
2. Close your eyes.
3. Pick a word, any word.
4. Say it again and again.

Since this is a "nonreligious" technique, the focus word doesn't need to be religious. I've seen the word "rock" mentioned as an example without any religious connotation, or even the brand name of a popular cola beverage. And since the technique is "nonreligious," it is open for all to benefit, regardless of what one believes or doesn't believe. Without the use of the usual eastern religious words or practices, it becomes devoid of any "religiosity" and becomes strictly a relaxation technique, with all of the health benefits previously noted. It's available for all and can be utilized regardless of belief system. Sounds great, doesn't it?

Frankly, I wouldn't buy into it so fast. I would offer the counter-opinion that it has been repackaged in such a way as to be more appealing to western tastes. And I would like to add the following impressions for further consideration:

You are practicing eastern meditation, whether you choose to call it eastern meditation or not.

By attempting to clear your mind of all thoughts the focus word that is repetitively used is a mantra, albeit a "nonreligious" one. The word used is unimportant (as noted previously). The fact that nonreligious or non-eastern words are used does not automatically make it a nonreligious relaxation technique. It is still eastern meditation in the sense that the main focus remains on emptying or clearing the brain (see the meditation model as discussed in chapter three). It would still be characterized as an eastern passive meditation technique, not an active technique as was noted with Christian meditation or Christian prayer. In other words, current scientific theory regarding the inner workings of the brain (i.e., the meditation model) would support a similar brain endpoint or peak meditative state regardless of the word used. (I would still call it a mantra.) At this brain endpoint, or peak meditative state, there is the theoretical darkening of both left and right orientation areas, resulting in an unlimited sense of self and space. These are the classic findings for eastern meditation (see the meditation model in chapter three). The end result is the same: eastern meditation. The word that is used in getting there has just been changed.

You are on the eastern religion pathway, whether you admit to eastern religious beliefs or not.

This "nonreligious" meditation technique is not "nonreligious" at all, but a repackaged version of classic eastern meditation. And eastern meditation is intricately linked with the eastern religions from which it came. We can again look at the following two quotes regarding Buddhism as an example: (1) "Buddhism teaches that meditation and the practice of good religious and moral behavior can lead to nirvana...."[49], and (2) "Meditation occupies a central place in Buddhism and combines, in its highest stages, the discipline of progressively increased introversion with the insight brought about by wisdom, or *prajna*."[50] As we can see, eastern meditation plays a major role, a "central place" within Buddhism. By regularly practicing this "nonreligious" eastern meditation to clear the mind, I would propose that you are still involved with an integral part of the eastern belief system. Although you may not admit to eastern religious beliefs consciously, I would suspect that you are being led in that direction. Thus, even if you do not believe in eastern theology, and use a "nonreligious" mantra in meditating strictly for relaxation purposes, it would seem that you are still wittingly or unwittingly on the eastern religion pathway.

Saying "Jesus" (or one of his teachings) repetitively as the focus word does not necessarily constitute a Christian prayer.

What about a "nonreligious" meditation in the above sense but saying "Jesus" (or one of his teachings) as the focus word that is said over and over again? Does this lead one closer to Christ? Could this suffice as a Christian type of prayer?

In considering these questions, the following definition of mantra is helpful: "A mantra is a phrase or word that you repeat to yourself (not out loud); it distracts you from other thoughts."[51] Thus, if the purpose of saying "Jesus" (or one of his teachings) is for distraction from other thoughts, then it would appear appropriate to consider it a type of mantra. Within this context, the goal is usually to clear the mind of all thoughts and to use the mantra in helping to achieve this. This again is classic eastern meditation, regardless of whether the focus word involves Jesus or not. Note that the main focus is on being distracted from other thoughts and clearing the mind; it is not on a deep contemplation of the mantra or the word itself. The mantra is a means to an end, not an end in itself. The fact that any word can be used as a mantra tells us it's not the word that counts but the process.

The problem with saying "Jesus" (or one of his teachings) as the mantra is that a mantra has a different purpose than praying to Jesus in the western sense (i.e., contemplating Christian truths, using scripture reading, prayerful personal communication, etc.). This instead is active Christian meditation or prayer (see the meditation model in chapter three or chapter five for clarification). A mantra is a means of clearing the brain of any thoughts, whereas Christian meditation and prayer involves filling the mind with Christ and his teachings. Within the Christian assumptions that have been taken for this book (see the end of chapter four), Jesus needs to be the main area of focus, not just a means of preventing distraction. Jesus needs to be the end and not the means.

Nonreligious Eastern Meditation Summary

Let's summarize this latter section regarding the nonreligious eastern meditation emphasis as follows: "Nonreligious" meditation remains religious in nature because it takes an essential part of eastern theology (eastern meditation) and repackages it according to western scientific emphasis and cultural taste. When the meditation model (as previously explained) is used, the end result of a nonreligious meditation would be the same as a more traditional eastern religious meditation. There is the same process of emptying or clearing the brain of all thoughts, perceptions, or emotions; the focus word (i.e., mantra) utilized in getting there has just been changed. Within the meditation model one would expect the same brain endpoint (i.e., peak meditative state) regardless of the mantra used. Even saying "Jesus" (or one of his teachings) as the mantra would not be expected to change the brain endpoint (i.e., peak meditative state) if the focus remains on a passive clearing of the brain rather than an active contemplation or prayer. Within the Christian assumptions that have been made for this book, Jesus needs to be the main area of focus and not just as a means of preventing distraction.

9 Just Another "High"?

Is there any possible relationship between eastern meditation and recreational drugs? Does a deep eastern meditation experience have any similarities with that achieved with mind-altering drugs? Could eastern meditation be considered a type of "high" without the use of recreational drugs? And what does any of this have to do with Christian prayer?

In addressing these possibilities, I would initially like to refer to our previous discussion involving TM. If you recall, we started the seventh chapter that introduced TM talking about the 1960s. The drug culture during that decade was highly visible within western society (especially the United States), with considerable use of recreational drugs among the youth. At that time there was marketing of TM as an alternative to illegal drug use. The goal was to encourage the use of TM to reduce dependence on these illegal drugs. It was this goal that partially contributed to the spread of TM throughout the public school system and into the U.S. Army.[52] Eastern meditation (in this case TM) grew during this time period with its initial scientific support and the perception that it could be a healthy alternative to illegal, mind-altering drugs.

In preparation for this book, I reviewed a considerable amount of information regarding eastern meditation. One common thread through much of the literature was the reference made to obtaining a heightened meditation experience. There is a frequent desire by individuals practicing eastern meditation to try to achieve deeper and deeper levels of meditation. The focus is often on having increasingly profound experiences. It is almost as if the goal is the ultimate in relaxation, the ultimate "high" without drugs.

One could counter: "But isn't Christian prayer similar? Isn't there also the focus to maximize one's Christian prayer?" Yes, however, in this context it is different. Based on the Christian assumptions that have been taken for this book (see the end of chapter four), Christian prayer does not seek to achieve this same type of ultimate "high." Christian prayer is by its very nature a relationship; it seeks an interpersonal closeness, not a maximum experience or event. I would define this difference between the two as follows: Eastern meditation is experiential as opposed to Christian prayer, which is interpersonal. Eastern meditation is characterized by an experience or happening involving the one meditating. Christian prayer, however, is characterized by a personal relationship between the individual and God. During the peak of the eastern meditation experience there is the loss of the sense of self as well as the loss of the sense of space. By definition the experience must involve only the individual who is meditating, as there is no other person involved. With Christian prayer, however, the personhood of both God and the individual is maintained. This unique and ongoing personal relationship with God is one of the core Christian teachings. (See chapter six for further review regarding this issue of personhood.)

While this eastern meditation "high" is experiential in nature, I further suggest that eastern meditation involves the seeking (intended or unintended) of an altered state of being. It is a type of escapism, a temporarily altered sense of one's individual self that is not unlike that attempted by recreational drug users. This, however, is not the case with Christian prayer. In Christian prayer the state of being is not changed; there is a firm grounding or stability of the sense of self (see chapter six again for reference).

Other similarities between eastern meditation and recreational or mind-altering drugs could be considered. We noted in chapter two that eastern meditation itself has also been associated with alterations within the brain. When practiced on a regular basis eastern meditation has resulted in brain wave changes that continue even during nonmeditating periods.[53] These ongoing brain wave changes would appear indicative of the effects of eastern meditation on the brain's electrical activity itself.

Along with these brain wave changes are brain chemical changes that have been documented. One very important brain neurotransmitter that is affected is serotonin.[54] Serotonin is the neurotransmitter that is associated with some forms of depression and anxiety. It is this relationship of serotonin to depression and anxiety that has triggered the huge use of the class of drugs known as selective serotonin reuptake inhibitors (SSRIs) including Prozac, Zoloft, and Paxil. An in-depth discussion of all of the biochemical changes that have been noted with eastern meditation is well beyond the purposes of this book.[55] The key point here is that eastern meditation itself is also mind-altering.

Thus, although eastern meditation has shown the above alterations within the brain, the question remains: "What about the side effects?" We initially discussed these physical and psychological side effects or adverse consequences associated with eastern meditation in chapter two. One study noted that 36 to 48 percent of long-term transcendental meditators had adverse effects.[56] A second, more comprehensive study involving Vipassana meditation noted a frequency of 38 to 55.5 percent in its long-term meditators. (Vipassana meditation is noted to be a quieting technique or mindfulness meditation developed in the Buddhist tradition in which one observes "whatever comes into awareness."[57]) In the first study, the side effects were only looked at retrospectively. In the second study, however, the side effects were looked at retrospectively and prospectively, after one month and six months. This monitoring for the second study followed an intensive Vipassana meditation retreat wherein the participants signed up for the study. In this second study the side effects were not only common but in some cases they were noted to be profoundly adverse.

The second study included some interesting descriptions of these side effects. At the one-month follow-up, one individual wrote that the meditation retreat left him completely disoriented, "confused, spaced out, quit meditating since retreat."[58] Another noted at the six-month follow-up:

> My experience of returning from the retreat was a difficult one. The mind set values that the retreat cultivated felt out of synch with the world I came back to and I've been slowly digesting the transformative changes that the retreat generated. Lots of depression, confusion, struggle during the last six months…experienced some severe shaking and energy releasing; eventually injured my back and stopped doing Vipassana practice.[59]

We can see in the above examples some of the side effects involving eastern meditation that were discussed in chapter two: confusion and disorientation, feeling "spaced out," depression, impaired reality testing, and dissociation (a sense of being separated or disconnected). The "severe shaking" noted in the second individual could be an example of the seizure-like activity that has been associated with eastern meditation. It could also be an example of a paradoxical increase in tension (the opposite of the relaxation that was expected) or an uncomfortable kinesthetic (bodily) sensation that has been noted (see chapter two to further review the descriptions of these terms).

There were even special problems with data collection in this second study. The following excerpt from a study participant is an example: "I am sorry to foul up your study, but I no longer feel able to make accurate generalizations about myself…one no longer knows 'what' one 'is' except in the moment—which makes filling out this form nigh impossible."[60] Again, we can see elements of depersonalization, a loss of the sense of one's own identity. And with this there can be the transition to psychosis-like symptoms with the loss of contact with reality, delusions, hallucinations, and finally despair. One last excerpt is quite explicit in this regard:

> One of my colleagues during the three month retreat was asked to leave early because he was becoming seriously unstable and delusive. Degeneration continued at home for a month and a half. Eventually he attempted suicide because he had "failed" to become enlightened. He is now hospitalized and is seriously mentally ill.[61]

As tragic and unfortunate as the above may be, however, there is still something further about these side effects that needs to be discussed. There is more to add about the above-noted studies, an important point that was found in both. That important point is this: the frequency of side effects increased in those who had meditated the longest. In other words, in both studies the longer-term meditators had the highest percentage of adverse effects. Empirically, one would suppose that the longer one meditated the better one would become at it, the more relaxed and with fewer side effects. The data, however, shows exactly the opposite. The longest meditation group of either study involved those in the second study. These were regular meditators of over an hour a day for an average of 105 months (almost nine years). In this group more than 75 percent reported adverse effects!

Based on these studies, therefore, the side effects are not only common but actually affect a large majority of longer-term meditators. And one could infer from this data that the longer one meditates, the greater the chance of developing side effects.

Should a person practice eastern meditation only to relax? Based on the aforementioned studies, I would say that person is playing with fire, possibly flirting with disaster. This is a potentially dangerous road. After all, there are many other ways to relax that don't have to involve the side effects discussed above. Proper nutrition, regular exercise, plenty of rest, going out in nature, and so forth could never be criticized. We know that studies involving laughter and humor have resulted in a number of health benefits. To be specific, laughter has a role in stress hormone reduction, improving mood, enhancing creativity, pain reduction, improving immunity, and reducing blood pressure.⁶² What about other methods of relaxation? What about watching a sunset? What about sitting quietly and knitting? What about working on a favorite hobby? Maybe medical science needs to refocus the research regarding healthy relaxation techniques further away from eastern meditation. Is it possible that the use of eastern meditation strictly as a relaxation technique could actually end up being just another fad, here today, gone tomorrow? In the end, only time will tell.

In conclusion, is eastern meditation just another "high"? As TM it was initially marketed as an alternative to illegal drugs in the 1960s and early 1970s. Was there simply the attempted replacement of one problem (illegal, recreational, mind-altering drugs) with yet another problem (eastern meditation—as TM), another "drug" of sorts? The proposed similarities of both eastern meditation and recreational drugs can be summarized as follows:

1. They are experiential in nature and not interpersonal (like Christian prayer).
2. They provide a type of escapism and can result in a temporarily altered state of being.
3. There are documented mind-altering changes (brain wave and brain chemical).
4. There are frequent and at times significantly adverse physical and psychological side effects.
5. The occurrence of side effects is increased with long-term use.

10 Spiritual Combat

A thick, haunting, eerie fog sets the tone at the beginning of the movie, *The Passion of the Christ*. The powerful scene opens in the Garden of Gethsemane. The figure of Jesus is seen in anguish, initially standing, at times kneeling. He is praying fervently to his Father in utter distress. The temptation that he suffers is symbolized by disparaging questions from the evil one. Clever serpentine semantics are used. "No one man can carry this burden…I tell you. It is far too heavy." The devil is portrayed as an androgynous figure, an actress with a shaved head and the deep voice of a man. "Saving their souls is too costly." "No one." "Ever." "No." "Never." A small underground earthen creature wriggles in the nose for added special effect. A snake is sent slithering toward Christ, to inflict its deadly bite. Jesus is sweating profusely, his entire being engrossed in this spiritual battle. He stands, steadies himself, and with one swift step crushes the head of the serpent…

Good versus evil. How could we know what good is if there isn't also the presence of evil? What would we compare it to? In chapter four we assumed that the

God of the Old Testament is indeed the true God, that Jesus is His Son, that Jesus is equal to the Father and "the way, the truth, and the life." If we take this assumption seriously, however, we must also conclude that the evil one exists as well. Otherwise, from what would Jesus be saving all mankind? Dealings with evil occur throughout Jesus' life. He is tempted three times in the desert before he even starts his public ministry, quoting Deuteronomy successive times in rebuttal (Matthew 4:1–11). He casts out devils (Matthew 8:16, 8:31, 9:33) and he criticizes Peter: "Get behind me, Satan!" (Matthew 16:23). Even in Christ's presence at the Last Supper, Judas was lost: "And during supper, when the devil had already put it into the heart of Judas Iscariot, Simon's son, to betray him…" (John 13:2). No, we cannot sugarcoat things. We cannot believe only in Jesus and pretend that the other side doesn't exist. We can't just pay attention to the good and ignore the bad. The evil one caused tragedy and disharmony during Jesus' time. If we take these assumptions seriously, then we must also acknowledge that he contributes to the disharmony and injustice of our current day.

So what does any of this have to do with eastern meditation? A concern with having the mind go "blank," with clearing out all thoughts, emotions, and perceptions from the mind is that it could place one at spiritual risk. Christ, in contrast, struggled with temptations while alone in the desert (see above, Matthew 4:1–11). The intensity of the experience was such that the angels came to his comfort afterward. We opened this chapter focusing on Jesus in the Garden of Gethsemane. He was in anguish, involved in intense prayer as he warded off temptation. He needed his full attention and strength whenever engaging in spiritual combat.

To practice eastern meditation, however, passively takes one into an unprotected spiritual void. It is different from Christian prayer. It takes one to a void that could be potentially dangerous and spiritually risky. It is a void without the supernatural guidance of Christ.

11 The Supernatural Flight

How, then, do we pull the information in this book together? How do we apply the noted scientific findings along with the spiritual concepts in an understandable fashion? What is our final conclusion?

I would like to propose a simple analogy. The analogy itself is imperfect, yet there are points that I think could be helpful. I would like to compare Christian prayer and eastern meditation to flying on a plane. First, let's look at Christian prayer. A Christian goes off to a quiet place to begin to pray. Once off at the quiet place, he reads some Bible verses or contemplates some of Christ's teachings. He closes his eyes and gets in a comfortable sitting position, or possibly a kneeling position as he focuses more and more on Christ and his teachings. This is, in a way, similar to a plane that is starting to get ready to take off. By being in a quiet place, not paying attention to outer surroundings, he is preparing for an inner journey. As his mind continues to focus, the plane begins to take off. His right brain attention area facilitates the right brain orientation area to intensify its contemplation on Christ. The plane is gaining speed. In the case of the Christian, the plane is flying at midday and is flying directly toward the sun. The sun is representative of Christ. As the plane flies closer to Christ, there is a change beyond Christian meditation to communication. There is the actual development of prayer. It is the essence of a personal communication with Christ as the plane approaches the direction of the sun. Therefore, with the Christian, there is not strictly Christian meditation but the option for deep contemplative prayer, which entails this actual communication with Christ.

Using the same analogy, however, yields significantly different results with eastern meditation. In this case, a person who is practicing eastern meditation will get into a plane and prepare for takeoff. He will sit in a quiet area, with legs crossed in the lotus or other position, where he will calm his mind. His right brain attention area will focus on calming down the brain's orientation areas as previously discussed. His eyes close, his focus turns inward. The plane begins to take off. In this case, however, the plane would be flying at night. Instead of approaching the sun, which represents Christ in the above analogy, the eastern meditator flies his plane up into the dark sky. There is nothing but blackness and unlimited space and time. There is no personal relationship or personal communication.

Now, cross that bridge of faith, as previously discussed, onto the other side. We are assuming that Jesus is indeed who he claimed to be. He is the Son of God, he is equal to God the Father, and he is "the way, the truth and the life." With this assumption in mind, how would it affect our interpretation of the eastern meditation analogy described above?

Yes, eastern meditation can lead to a sense of relaxation, but at what risks? These risks could be considered potential turbulence on the aforementioned flight. There are the physical and psychological adverse side effects that can wreak havoc. The more frequently this flight is taken, the greater the chances appear of running into this type of disruption. There are also the spiritual risks, a significant danger when flying into unprotected spiritual territory. Body, mind, and soul, all at risk as the flight proceeds into the dark night…

Where is this eastern meditation flight really going? I suggest the following: It is on a pathway leading not to the Light of the World but to the darkness of nothingness. It is an impersonal trip to nowhere as opposed to an ever-personal relationship with the All Loving and All Knowing God. No matter where it goes, it does not take one to the Lord Jesus Christ.

NOTES

[1] *Christianity, Cults, and Religions.* Torrance, California: Rose Publishing, Inc., 1994.

[2] *The HarperCollins Dictionary of Religion.* The American Academy of Religion, 1995.

[3] "History and Comparison of Major Religions." www.greatdreams.com/religin4.htm.

[4] *The New Encyclopedia Britannica,* vol. 2, 2002.

[5] www.mindandlife.org.

[6] Perez-De-Albeniz, Alberto, and Jeremy Holmes. "Meditation: Concepts, Effects, and Uses in Therapy." *International Journal of Psychotherapy* 5:1 (March 2000): 49–59.

[7] *Real Simple* (May 2004): 141.

[8] *Time* (4 August 2003).

[9] Benson, Herbert. *The Relaxation Response.* New York: Avon, 1975.

[10] Jevning, R., R. K. Wallace, and M. Beidebach. "The Physiology of Meditation: A Review. A Wakeful Hypometabolic Integrated Response." *Neuroscience and Biobehavioral Reviews* 16 (1992): 415–442; Sudsuang, R., V. Chentanez, and K. Vluvan. "Effect of Buddhist Meditation on Serum Cortisol and Total Protein Level, Blood Pressure, Pulse Rate, Lung Volume and Reaction Time." *Physiology and Behavior* 50 (1991): 545–548.

[11] Bairey-Murrs, Noelle. *Star Magazine* (1 February 2004).

[12] Anand, B. K., G. S. China, and B. Singh. "Some Aspects of Electroencephalographic Studies on Yogis." *Electroencephalography and Clinical Neurophysiology* 13 (1961): 452–456; Banquet, J. P. "EEG and Meditation." *Electroencephalography and Clinical Neurophysiology* 33 (1972): 454; Corby, J. C., et al. "Psychophysiological Correlates of the Practice of Tantric Yoga Meditation." *Archives of General Psychiatry* 35 (1978): 571–577; Benson, H., et al. "Three Case Reports of the Metabolic and Electroencephalographic Changes During Advanced Buddhist Meditation Techniques." *Behavioral Medicine* 16 (1990): 90–95.

[13] Solberg, E. E., et al. "Meditation: A Modulator of the Immune Response to Physical Stress? A Brief Report." *British Journal of Sports Medicine* 29 (1995): 255–257; Davidson, R. J., et al. "Alterations in Brain and Immune Function Produced by Mindfulness Meditation." *Psychosomatic Medicine* 65 (2003): 564–570.

[14] Rosenfeld, Isadore. *Dr. Rosenfeld's Guide to Alternative Medicine.* New York: Random House, 1996.

[15] Shapiro, D. H. "Adverse Effects of Meditation; a Preliminary Investigation of Long-Term Meditators." *International Journal of Psychosomatics* 39 (1992): 62–67.

[16] Craven, J. L. "Meditation and Psychotherapy." *Canadian Journal of Psychiatry* 34 (1989): 648–653.

[17] Kutz, I., J. K. Burysenko, and H. Benson. "Meditation and Psychotherapy: A Rationale for the Integration of Dynamic Psychotherapy, the Relaxation Response and Mindfulness Meditation." *American Journal of Psychiatry* 142 (1985a): 1–8.

[18] *The Various Implications Arising from the Practice of Transcendental Meditation: An empirical analysis of pathogenic structures as an aid in counseling.* Bensheim, Germany: Institute for Youth and Society, 1980.

[19] Rothenberg, M., and F. Chapman. *Dictionary of Medical Terms for the Nonmedical Person*, 4th edition. Barron's Educational Series, Inc., 2000.

[20] Castillo, Richard J. "Depersonalization and Meditation." *Psychiatry: Interpersonal and Biological Processes* (May 1990): 158–169.

[21] *Merck Manual*, 17th edition. Merck & Co., 1999.

[22] Persinger, Michael A. "Transcendental meditation and general meditation were associated with enhanced complex partial epileptic-like signs: evidence for 'cognitive kindling'?" *Perceptual and Motor Skills* (1993).

[23] Markides, K. S. "Aging, Religiosity, and Adjustment: A Longitudinal Analysis." *Journal of Gerontology* 38 (1983): 621–625; Koenig, H. G. "Religious behaviors and death anxiety in later life." *The Hospice Journal* 4:1 (1988): 3–24; Koenig, H. G., et al. "Religious practices and alcoholism in a southern adult population." *Hospital and Community Psychiatry* 45:3 (1994).

[24] Keonig, H. G., et al. *Is Religion Good for Your Health? The Effects of Religion on Physical and Mental Health.* New York: The Hayworth Pastoral Press, 1997.

[25] Ibid.

[26] Neeleman, J., and R. Persaud. "Why Do Psychiatrists Neglect Religion?" *British Journal of Medical Psychology* 68 (June 1995): 169–178.

[27] Newberg, A., and E. D'Aquili. *Why God Won't Go Away: Brain Science and the Biology of Belief.* New York: Ballantine Books, 2001.

[28] Newberg, A., and E. D'Aquili. *Zygon* 28 (1993): 177–200; Newberg, A., and E. D'Aquili. *The Mystical Mind: Probing the Biology of Religious Experience.* Minneapolis: Fortress Press, 1999.

[29] See note 27 above.

[30] All biblical quotations are excerpted from the Revised Standard Version.

[31] Carus, Paul. *Buddha, The Gospel.* Chicago: Open Court Publishing Company, 1894.

[32] Ibid.

[33] *Buddha, The Word: The Eightfold Path*, c. 500 B.C.

[34] See note 31 above.

[35] See note 31 above.

[36] Littleton, C. Scott. *The Sacred East.* Berkeley, California: Seastone, 1999.

[37] See note 31 above.

[38] Melton, J. Gordon. *Encyclopedic Handbook of Cults in America.* New York: Garland Publishing, 1986.

[39] Ibid.

[40] Lazarus, Arnold A. "Psychiatric Problems Precipitated by Transcendental Meditation." *Psychology Reports* (1976): 601–602.

[41] "New High from the Maharishi: Levitation from Meditation; the Maharishi's New High." *Washington Post* 6 June 1977: B-1.

[42] "Excerpts from the affidavit of John W. Patterson." www.unstress4less.org/transcendental_meditation-tmresearch-problems.htm.

[43] Gardner, Martin. "Notes of a Fringe Watcher—Doug Henning and the Giggling Guru." *The Skeptical Enquirer* (May/June 1995). http://www.cskop.org/si/9505/tm.html.

[44] Kropinski, Robert. United States District Court for the District of Columbia. Civil Suit #85-2848, 1986.

[45] *The Philadelphia Enquirer* (14 January 1987).

[46] Roark, Dennis E. *TM-Ex Newsletter* (Spring 1992). http://minet.org/TM-EX/Spring-92.

47 See note 38 above.
48 *The Kansas City Star* (25 September 2004): F-14.
49 See note 3 above.
50 See note 4 above.
51 See note 14 above.
52 See note 38 above.
53 Khare, K. C., and S. K. Nigam. "A study of electroencephalogram in meditators." *Indian Journal of Physiology and Pharmacy* 44:2 (April 2002): 173–178; Delmonte, M.M. Electrocortical Activity and Related Phenomenon Associated with Meditation Practice: A Literature Review." *International Journal of Neuroscience* 24:3–4 (November 1984): 217–231.
54 Bujatti, M., and P. Riederer. "Serotonin, noradrenaline, dopamine metabolites in transcendental meditation-technique." *International Journal of Neuroscience* 39:3 (1976): 257–267.
55 For more information about biochemical changes during meditation, see: O'Halloran, J. P., et al. "Hormonal control in a state of decreased activation: potentiation of arginine vasopressin secretion." *Physiological Behavior* 35:4 (October 1985): 591–595; Infante, J. R., et al. "ACTH and Beta-Endorphin in Transcendental Meditation." *Physiological Behavior* 64:3 (June 1998): 311–315; Jevning, R., H. C. Pirkle, and A. F. Wilson. "Behavioral Alteration of Plasma Phenylalanine Concentration." *Physiological Behavior* 19:5 (November 1977): 611–614; Kesterson, John, and Noah F. Clinch. "Increased Carbon Dioxide (Metabolic Rate, Respiratory Exchanged Ratio and Apneas) During (TM) Meditation." *The American Journal of Physiology* (March 1989): R637.
56 Otis, L. S. "Adverse effects of transcendental meditation." *Meditation: Classic and Contemporary Perspectives*. D. H. Shapiro and R. N. Walsh, Eds. New York: Aldine, 1984.
57 See note 15 above.
58 See note 15 above.
59 See note 15 above.
60 See note 15 above.
61 See note 15 above.
62 *Australian Family Physician* 30:1 (January 2001): 25–28.

INDEX

A

American Heart Association 8

B

Beatles, The 47
Benson, Herbert 8
Bible 18, 19
   New Testament 36-37
   Old Testament 31-36
Brahman. *See* God
British Journal of Medical Psychology 14-15
Buddha 5, 28, 29-30
   doctrines of 5
Buddha, The Gospel 30, 35-36, 38, 44
Buddhism 4-5, 6-7, 27, 36, 55, 58. *See also* Hinduism
   claims of 4, 4-5, 27, 55

C

Christian prayer. *See* Prayer, Christian
Christianity 14, 19, 24, 26, 45
   exclusiveness of 31-35, 37-39
   moral truths of 31

D

Dalai Lama 6-7, 27
D'Aquili, Eugene, M.D., Ph.D. 17-18, 20
Devil, the 70
Drugs 62, 63, 64, 69
Dylan, Bob 46

E

Eastern meditation. *See* Meditation, eastern
Encyclopedic Handbook of Cults in America 52-53

F

"fight or flight" 8

G

Garden of Gethsemane 70
God 3, 4, 18, 25, 32, 33, 34, 35, 37, 40, 42, 43, 64, 75
God, chosen people of 32-35
   Abraham 32
   Moses 32-34, 36-37
   Noah 32
God of the Old Testament 34, 36, 38, 71
Guru Dev 47

H

Harrison, George 47-48
Hinduism 4, 4-5, 27, 55

I

International Journal of Psychotherapy 7
Is Religion Good for Your Health? The Effects of Religion on Physical and Mental 12

J

Jesus Christ 22, 24, 25, 26, 36, 40, 41, 60, 70, 72, 74
   baptism of 37
   claims by 24-27
John the Baptist 37

K

Koenig, Harold, M.D. 12

L

Last Supper, the 71
Lord's Prayer, The 41

M

Maharishi Mahesh Yogi 46-49
Mantra 1, 19, 47, 55, 57, 59, 60, 61
   definition of 59-60
Meditation, and prayer similarities of 1-3
Meditation, Buddhist 6
Meditation, Christian 42
   active 22-23

Meditation, depersonalization in 11, 67
Meditation, eastern 1, 2, 16, 21, 24, 39, 44, 53, 54, 55, 56, 58, 63, 64, 66, 71, 74
   adverse side effects of 9-11, 65-68
   and seizure-like activity 10-11, 66
   health benefits of 4-11
   possible relationship to recreational drugs 62-69
   passive 20-21
Meditation, effects of on body 8-9
Meditation, four steps of 7-8, 56-57
Meditation, scientific model of 17-23, 44-45
   and Christian perspective 40-42
Meditation, Vipassana 65-66
Meditators, Tibetan study of 17-23. *See also* Nuns
Mehesh Prasad Varma 46-47. *See* Maharishi Mahesh Yogi
Metabolic syndrome 8
Mind and Life Institute, The 6-7, 27, 55

N

National Institutes of Health 9
   Office on Alternative Medical Systems and Practice 9
Neurotheology 2-3, 27

INDEX

Newberg, Andrew, M.D. 17-18, 20
Nirvana 5, 29, 44
Nuns, Franciscan
  study of 17. *See also* Meditators, Tibetan: study of

O

Office on Alternative Medical Systems and Practice 9

P

Passion of the Christ, The 70
Paxil 65
Personhood 2, 43-45, 64
  definition of 43
Pontius Pilate 26
Prayer, and meditation
  similarities of 1-3
Prayer, Christian 64, 69, 72, 73
  adverse side effects of 14-16
  health benefits of 11-20
Prozac 65
Psychiatry, and religion
  gap between 15
PsychINFO 13
Pubmed 13

R

Real Simple 7
Relaxation Response, The 8
Religion, and psychiatry
  gap between 15

S

Sanskrit 5, 6, 55
Selective serotonin reuptake inhibitors (SSRIs) 65
Siddhartha Gautama 4-5
Single photon emission computerized tomography (SPECT) 17-20
Skeptical Enquirer 50-51
Son of God 24, 26, 38, 75
Supernatural 3, 36, 37, 72, 73

T

Time 8
Transcendental Meditation (TM) 2, 47-50, 52, 54, 56, 69
  arrival of in western world 46-53
  as an alternative to illegal drug use 62
  controversy in 55
  decline in popularity of 54-61
  spinoffs of 54-61
    traditional eastern religion emphasis 55
    nonreligious eastern meditation emphasis 56-61
Transcendental Meditation movement 46-49

U

U.S. Army 62

83

W

Washington Post 49
Why God Won't Go Away: Brain Science and the Biology of Belief 17-18

Woodstock 46
World Plan Executive Council 48

Z

Zoloft 65

Give the Gift of
PRAYER OR MANTRA?
A Contrast Between Christian Prayer and Eastern Meditation
to Your Friends and Colleagues

CHECK YOUR LEADING BOOKSTORE OR ORDER HERE

❏ **YES**, I want _____ copies of *Prayer or Mantra?* at $11.95 each, plus $4.95 shipping per book. (Ohio residents please add 87¢ sales tax per book.) Canadian orders must be accompanied by a postal money order in U.S. funds. Allow 15 days for delivery.

My check or money order for $_____ is enclosed.

Please charge my: ❏ Visa   ❏ MasterCard
                  ❏ Discover   ❏ American Express

Name _____

Organization _____

Address _____

City/State/Zip _____

Phone_____ Email _____

Card # _____

Exp. Date_____ Signature _____

Please make your check payable and return to:

Seventy-Three Publications
c/o Bookmasters, Inc. Fulfillment Svcs.
30 Amberwood Parkway, Ashland, OH 44805

Call your credit card order toll-free to 800-247-6553

fax 419/281-6883   e-mail: order@bookmasters.com

www.prayerormantra.com